THE FIRST TIME
Manager

*Your crash course in effective
leadership and management*

VICTORIA SCOTT

TABLE OF CONTENT

INTRODUCTION

More than half of new managers fail in their first year. No one tells you this when you move into management, whether it's a team of two or jumping the ranks to manage a group of 50, 100, or more.

What we often remember is a feeling of elation, of having 'made it'. The good news call to loved ones and friends, the congratulatory dinner and glass of champagne. The perception is that moving up the corporate ladder is *exciting*, but most first-time managers will tell a different story.

This book is designed to be a driver's manual for your first time in the manager's seat. You may read it in one go, but like most things in the business world, you learn from doing. Some topics we discuss may go over your head, some may make you laugh or question whether you really need to know it – but every manager's journey is a learning one. I hope that you will turn to this as a reference while you develop on this path and carve out a space for yourself as a leader and a successful part of any management team you enter.

This book will cover both execution and mental strategies to conquer the skills and traits you will need to develop as a manager.

WHAT THE RIGHT EXPECTATIONS ARE

Expectations as a First Time Manager

Having the right internal expectations and dialogue is key to helping you navigate the ups and downs of management. Much like entrepreneurship, you are unlikely to go through a training school, have a handbook, or for most managers, have a mentor to guide you through mistakes and successes.

Management is more often than not, mentally exhausting and draining.

You make the switch from thinking about yourself,to being responsible for a team, department, and company on a larger scale of operations and results. Depending on how high you climb, you are also now responsible for managing the well-being, internal reputation and performance of yourself with little to no pat on the back.

For first-time managers, I encourage them to develop what is termed as 'the Entrepreneurs Mindset.' In any situation or challenge that arises, think to yourself – How would I feel or deal with this, if it were my business? This allows you to remove emotion and bias from a situation and look towards a shared goal and success.

The higher you climb, the less recognition you can expect, you will instead be exposed to increased criticism and back-seat-management. Exactly like the back-seat driver, every person in your team and company will assume they have the ability to do it better, to have solutions or answers that seem obvious after-the-fact.

Learning to understand the criticism is inevitable:, you are now in a position that encourages criticism (hindsight bias is strong), and you *will* need to be your own biggest cheerleader, helping you drive through the eventual down periods.

Never expecting a pat on the back, but achieving success and fulfillment from results will be the new normal.

UNDERSTANDING YOUR RESPONSIBILITIES

Whether it's mid or upper-management, moving into management means one thing, switching from the employee side to company side.

You now represent the company you work for at a higher level; your team will be looking to you for direction, stability, and growth.

A manager's key duties can be split into two main areas: short-term and long-term.

Short-term is the day to day operations of working in the business. Long-term are higher-level, higher-value, and tend to be focused on strategy and innovation. These are activities that help the company scale and grow. Whether you want to be a good manager, a great manager, or be seen as a leader, balancing the day to day with moving the department and company forward is vital.

A good manager will manage their team and their area and ensure everything is functioning.

A leader will drive performance results and company profit and growth forward.

A good manager does not need to be a Leader immediately, but a leader must know the fundamentals of a good manager to be one, and in the future, groom and develop a team of managers (as you move up the ranks to an executive, C-Suite or even entrepreneur/business owner).

Common Mistakes as a First Time Manager

You will face criticism, and you will make mistakes. Making decisions for the company with various people at different levels involved will always spur a difference of opinion. You do not necessarily need the respect or trust of your team to perform and deliver well, however having it does make your job and management life easier.

Being aware of the three areas below will help you minimize creating distrust in your team and help minimize emotional and political obstacles in your management growth.

Inconsistency

As with anything new, it's hard to know everything at once. Perhaps you have come into a new company or moved into the company after ten years; all scenarios require adjustment.

You will feel under pressure to perform, which can lead to making poor decisions.

Going back and forth or changing your approach with little communication can come off as being inconsistent.

Stand your ground when making decisions, and move fast but gather the information required and keep a cool head to think without rashness.

Fake It Till You Make It – the Wrong Way

If you have risen to a management position, prepare to face opponents that challenge your status. Learning to build confidence and kill self-doubt is what you need to survive.

Like with any new skill, expertise comes with time, and you will need to fake it till you make it.

Be wary of failing to ask your team when needed and when to appear vulnerable. No manager can operate alone, and your team does not expect you to.

Learning to Lead vs. Manage

If you want to progress beyond a good manager to a leader, you will need to learn to 'run towards the fire.' A saying I often use in management coaching, all rational humans run from danger. A manager is the front-line for dealing with crises, and instead of running you must seek 'fires'.

Choosing to ignore or let someone else deal with issues that affect the company is no longer an option.

THE ESSENTIALS FOR FIRST TIME MANAGERS

I received a letter of intent to sue on behalf of the company, just a year and a half into my management career. At this point, I was managing a team of 80, interviewing and hiring over 300 people, and I still made a rookie mistake.

I had decided to give a staff member a chance after feeling like they weren't a fit and when it turned out I was right, I gave them a days' notice (within their probationary period) that it wouldn't work out. Within the labor laws, every staff member needs 30 days notice at any stage of their probation period which is typically 90 days.

I knew this, and yet I still forgot. Luckily I managed to resolve the issue swiftly with a steep $3000 fee. And did I mention the intention letter was in a foreign language and the delivery person needed a signature of acceptance, effectively giving them the right to take me to court.

You can make mistakes in your career at any stage during your management journey; it's an ongoing battle between doing the best you can, and keeping your head up to continue forward. No matter which position or industry you are in, the essentials still stand.

We are going to cover hiring your team, developing your team, and nurturing a high performing culture (a skill in itself).

BUILDING A HIGH PERFORMING TEAM

There are two ways to build a team:

1. The type of people you want to work with – attitude fit

2. The type of people that are needed – opportunity fit

Both ways are neither correct nor incorrect.

I strongly believe in identifying traits or attitude markers to start establishing a culture right from hiring. You will, however, need to remain unbiased and always focused on the company.

You may be hiring a Sales Manager. Let's say your potential candidate's name is Adam. Adam might have all the skills and background, but is a bit bold and will clash with some of the team members in marketing. He may not be a 10/10 attitude-wise, but he has the potential to grow the business and be groomed to get along with the team.

In this case, do you prioritize attitude or opportunity fit? The answer, in this case, should be a bit of both You should identify that:

1. Attitude Fit = 5/10

2. Opportunity Fit = 8/10

You hire Adam.

Your Hiring Toolbox

A few things can make hiring a breeze.

Identify your different persona's. (What is the company DNA, and how do you identify it in the people joining your team?)

Have a strong hiring and testing process to match your company culture and expectations.

Have grading scales in place to remove bias and improve volume while maintaining consistency.

HOW TO MANAGE PEOPLE

Being a manager is like being a builder. Having the right tools at your disposal won't ensure you create a quality product. But it's better than not having any tools at all.

In this section, we will navigate some practices (tools) you can learn to adapt to the situations you will need to face quickly. Finding your style, building your management persona, and developing yourself as a manager is something you can only do in the real world and not through words on a sheet.

Having Staff Follow Policy

It all becomes your responsibility. When you step into the manager's shoes, there is no more them or I (unfortunately), your boss and your bosses' boss are now looking at you to be the fixer. It can be overwhelming; you are directly responsible for the actions and decisions your team makes.

A simple technique to ensure minimal negative consequences can be applying the 4W approach to staff management.

Who – is responsible in the situation?

What – is the policy and what action do they need to take?

Where – are the scenarios of the policy?

Why – are the potential repercussion of not following policy and what decisions should you take?

You need to systemize both behavior and decision making.

Step 1: Outline the policy and set up the correct communications and consequence models for the above.

Step 2: Monitoring, like with any process, system, or new team policy, you must have several communication and monitoring methods in place to ensure a full 360-degree rollout.

Let's say that you need every staff member to wash their hands before entering the office.

The successful outcome is [staff members are washing their hands, staff members washing their hands are recorded; if a staff member does not wash their hands, there are behavioral repercussions]. As a manager, you might put the following in place:

- A communications document and signs around the wash station to announce the new policy.

- Hold a meeting to ensure the document is understood, and staff understands the new policy as well as the repercussions if the new policy is not followed (and how the manager will be notified.

- A soap dispenser with a timer that records every time the dispenser is used.

- A senior member checks the soap dispenser log daily for any staff who have skipped this action. The first three strikes result in extra work duties. After three, they receive a verbal / written warning that goes into their file.

In this scenario, you ensure all 4W's are met – but this does not build a great culture or a great team, it just gets the job done in the most basic way.

Managing Internal Politics

I remember sitting down two of my employees separately in crisis intervention. They were both heads of departments causing conflict within each of their teams because the two couldn't get along. One was a long time team member with a huge ego but also one of the highest performing (and smartest) team members in the company. But he could not step out of the employee pattern and into the entrepreneurship mindset to see that his actions were impacting the greater good of the company.

The intervention proved less than fruitful. The senior employee chose not to acknowledge his part in the total lack of teamwork, and we ended up terminating him shortly after this issue because the politics and financial impact on the company grew too large.

There is one golden rule I go back to when it comes to manager coaching that works in any scenario – people are people. We tend to overcomplicate situations, make assumptions about others, and close off. But, at the end of the day, we are dealing with people in unique situations, who have feelings, flaws, strengths, and weaknesses. Politics within your teams can ruin a business. It causes people to ignore issues, become disengaged, and make poor decisions. In many cases, you need to identify and solve politics quickly and correctly.

Take a four-step scenario development approach:

1. Assess the impact/driving forces–how many people are involved, and how long has it been happening?

2. Isolate the reasons–what situations may have caused these reactions?

3. Identify the uncertainties–is there additional information required for you to formulate the next actions?

4. Identify and execute the actions–move swiftly and take specific steps based on the potential scenario paths.

Let's take three different scenarios and apply the scenario development approach:

1. Greg and Sam work on the Sales team, and because they have the same objectives (sales targets) and because Sam shows aggressiveness by taking some sales first, they have been butting heads. The issue has grown with no resolution in sight.

2. Greg and Amy work in two different cross-functional departments. Amy often works with Greg to coordinate projects, but Greg is not good at pro-actively communicating his work requirements,causing mistakes and the blame is placed on them both.

3. Susan and Amy are two senior workers and both high performers. They run in different work circles, and while their work is not directly related, their two teams would benefit from a closer relationship.

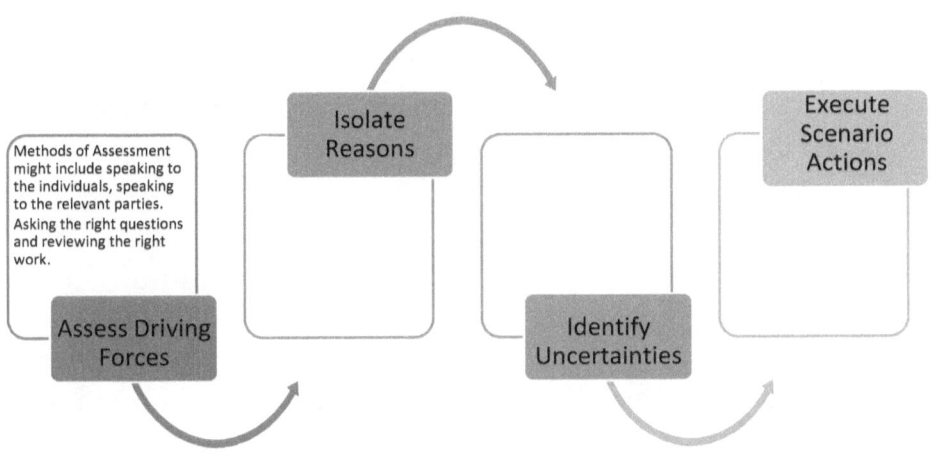

Having Successful Discussions & Structuring Communication

Imagine your team is like goldfish; they have limited listening and memory ability. Why does this help? Because it teaches you the importance of having strong communication and delivery skills. You will require communication skills across multiple aspects of management.

Let's say you hand a project off to a member of your team; you expect that they will set up meetings, organize the project ,and provide a follow-up report. None of this happens.Why? This is due to poor communication and poor delegation. This failed outcome loses time and, ultimately, money for the business.

Communication scenarios may include growth and development discussions, disciplinary discussions or change, and behavioral management. You have different levels of communication; it may be to an individual or a team of 500. At each of these levels, you need to adapt your speaking style, while keeping the building blocks the same. Communication is used to enact change – we communicate as managers to outline expectations, manage expectations, and align on outcomes. You can take these models and apply them to large scale project talks, brief emails, or 5-minute conversations.

Lewin's Three Stage Change Model is one that you can use in any communication scenario.

Elevating you from good to great as a manager and leader means you must also take emotional delivery into your speaking. You are dealing with people, whether it's a few or amassed over many departments. Remembering that when it comes to communication it is *never* about you, but about the outcome you deliver. This means keeping emotions neutral, using facts, not bias, and keeping your statements clear, concise, and structured so that your staff can easily take away key points.

Being long-winded, nervous, or rambling is not about you – but simply being a poor manager. As a first-time supervisor, you may lack confidence or experience moments of self-doubt, but your focal point is always pushing the company forward. Poor communication lets down your staff and leads to stagnation.

Reference:

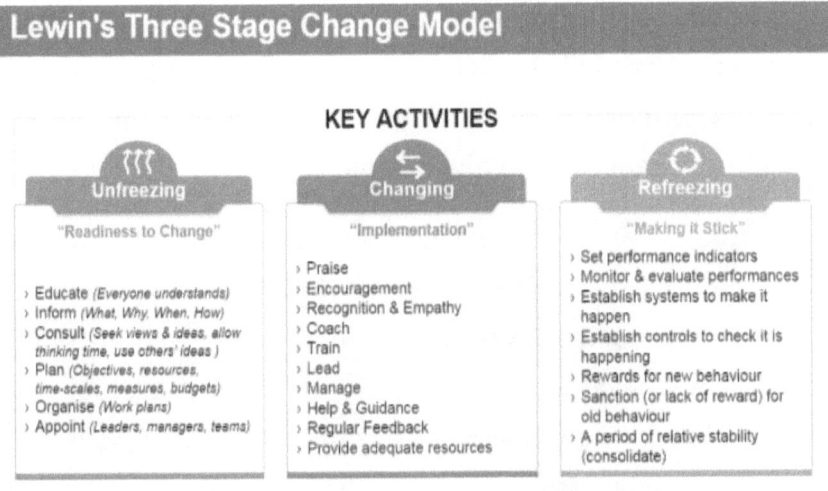

How to Manage a Negative Employee With Attitude Restructuring

You turn up to work excited because your team has continuously complained about the amount of paperwork they need to complete when filing a new sale. You have started to move the system online, which will cut 20 minutes off each sale, help the team's efficiency, and reduce data error. You are excited to deliver this news t because you know how much easier their lives will be. You set a morning meeting to run through the new online system and demo the upgraded sale protocol.

You look around expecting smiles when one staff member pipes up, "why do we need to fill this part in? It seems like it will waste so much time." A part of you is surprised, don't they see what you see, that the old system took *more* time – and this is better? Unfortunately, attitude in your team can be a common issue. People are plagued with emotions, clouded views, and attitude bias that they have no control over most of the time.

As soon as you spot this in your team, it needs to be fixed right away. Team members who display a negative attitude, go against the grain (not in the benefit of the group or company) can spread toxicity causing larger culture changes that will eventually need to be adjusted.

Typically the fastest way of dealing with an attitude restructure is a one-on-one with the staff member in question. Always come into a discussion with an employee with a solution-focused attitude. The meeting should never feel personal; it's just about two people coming up with a solution to a problem. The problem? Their negative attitude. This seemingly small issue can impact the business down the road, and both of you need to resolve it.

1. Acknowledge the issue – take specific examples and discuss why they were negative.

2. Reject excuses – show empathy and genuine care about the team member and the importance of changing the behavior, always outlining why it is not acceptable.

3. Force positive behavior – be very clear in the changes you expect to see and make the employee part of the solution; nobody enjoys criticism. In this case, you need to get the employee on your side as quickly as possible.

4. Set a timeline for change – you need to move quickly before allowing the team member to turn against you, the team, and the company (this shows immaturity in letting the issue get personal). Set expected timelines and follow up meetings and be prepared that if this toxicity continues you may need to let

this team member go.

Lastly, assess the impact and understand the difference between a problematic employee who needs support vs. a negative employee who is toxic. These two situations should be dealt with differently and met with empathy – your role as a manager is never to get frustrated, but rather be result-orientated in helping everyone and everything move forward.

Managing Salary Discussions

Typically for mid-sized companies, you may not have an HR team or a dedicated compensation team. Even if you are with a company that has rules regarding annual reviews, yearly pay rises and pay brackets, people tend to be sensitive when it comes to money. The best approach is to remove the direct link between money and value of the employee and very quickly tie the value of the employee to the larger picture which includes compensation, growth path, and work scope.

Many staff can be tied to salary, which is the base income you receive. Depending on your country, this may be weekly, monthly, or annually. However, managers should be aware of the big picture, and that is compensation. Compensation includes not just salary but all benefits that this team member receives.

Compensation benefits include things like additional extra annual leave (vacation days), bonus payments, remote workability, and so on. As an example, your salary base is $40,000 a year, but your additional benefits come to $15,000 per year, making your yearly compensation at the value of $55,000. For many, the focus is purely take-home pay or money in their pocket, but others vary, and you may need to change your approach in what they consider a value trade-off in regards to their perceived value to the company.

The company will sometimes set your compensation model, or you may not be fully in control of how much autonomy you have to give raises or give additional benefits. This section will provide an idea of how to navigate conversations and factors to take into consideration to avoid team members having negative feelings around compensation and turning into escalations down the track.

Standard Compensation Models:

1. Based on annual reviews

2. Based on performance/goals/KPIs

Commissions vs. non-commission based roles

Other factors may include salary benchmarking across industry standards or internal benchmarking, pay scale, and skill scale.

You may have compensation that is set up like this:

Scott is a software engineer who has been working at the company for two years has one additional year of experience prior but, came into the company at the base level.

1. Scott's base salary is $45,000 per year. Based on his skills and experience, we rank him as a Level 2 software engineer (with Level 6 being advanced).

2. The company has a pay scale that informs us a Level 2 software engineer is typically paid $38,000-$42,000. This means that Scott earns 7% above the max level for his level. He is at the higher end of his pay scale, and to get an increase, he needs to move up in scope, responsibility, and skill.

3. We discuss with Scott that we want him to gain the skills to move up to a Level 3 software engineer in 12 months, in which the pay bracket (you may keep this information internally and use data points or percentages instead, to set expectations accurately) is $40,000-$58,000.

4. However, Scott is expecting an increase this year based on his performance. In this case, instead of a base salary increase, you may set performance targets in his role to increase his yearly or quarterly compensation based on results. Scott may be working on a project that typically has 500 users with an average spend of $250 per year, resulting in $125,000 per year. You set a goal with Scott if he can increase usage of the project users to 650 users this year or increase the current user set to spend $162,500 he receives an additional month's bonus.

This achieves two things, you are upskilling Scott and retaining him in the company by demonstrating his growth path over the next 12 months , and pushing out a salary increase as he is already at the top tier for his level but tying an additional increase to a performance-based outcome.

Frequency of Conversations

As a manager, you set the frequency of conversations around this. You may have weekly check-in's, monthly one-on-ones, quarterly, or annual formal performance reviews. You tie all of this together in your conversations, your gradings, goals to set targets, and expectations aligned with compensation or promotion outcomes. In any case, you should make sure that every conversation is documented or clearly communicated with the employee, so you do not enter a scenario where the employee is expecting a promotion or increase in 6 months which was never discussed.

Navigating Promotions

Having benchmarks in place of what you expect of team members at various levels allows you to have the right levers for promotion discussions. Unfortunately, most promotions happen out of necessity, with employees thrown into senior roles because they are required vs. being the best fit. Where possible, this should be avoided. Not only does it put the wrong person in position, but it also sets the wrong example to other staff members around growth in the company.

This can't always be avoided, so we will tackle both scenarios of a planned promotion vs. promotions out of necessity.

Promotions out of Necessity

Promotions out of necessity occur for different reasons. You might have a very small team (say four people in a company), a manager or senior staff member leaves with short notice with responsibility and accountability that needs to be filled quickly. You have a growing young or inexperienced team, and you need to pick the most senior person (maybe that person has been with the company for eight months compared to the other staff members at four months) as the company is growing rapidly.Leadership or hierarchy is required (sometimes a good business problem to have).

When promotions out of necessity happen, this is a quick learning experience for everyone in the company. You will have some staff members that thrive, but some that never really step into the role. Pushing hard with challenges, targets, and balancing that with coaching and support planned promotions will yield higher profits in the long run.

Staff Growth – Developing Staff & Specialist Tracks

Retaining staff helps scalability of a business, and scalability allows cash flow, profit, and profit margins. It's a win-win; you keep staff and knowledge in the business, reduce training time, and invest in a team that continues to give back. You will churn staff without keeping an eye on retention, which leads to increased time on hiring, onboarding, and training. An average staff member can take 100 hours of training or the equivalent of up to $2000.

I remember an incredibly tough time in the business with a high turnover of our client services team, almost 70%. Still not as bad as a counterpart we heard had 100% turnover at that time. This means if you have 100 team members the first year, by the second, you might still have 100 team members, but they would be new faces. It stifles the growth of the business from all levels, upper management, mid-management, team dynamics, and morale.

Nurturing your existing staff and getting ahead of staff churn through staff growth is key to growing a healthy, engaged team, ultimately leading to higher performance. It also helps you as a manager. Keeping knowledge capital within the unit reduces the knowledge and mistake gaps you need to look out for. Staff churn can be directly related to workplace mistakes, and in our case there is an increase in client churn (money going down the drain.) When it comes to staff growth and development, I always say that retention starts on day one. What does that mean? From when you first engage with that potential employee, your role in retaining that staff member has begun. You are frontloading the work to ensure a pay-off in 12 months or longer from good hiring, onboarding, and development. You should be inbuilding development paths and growth discussions into the lifecycle of the employee.

How to Identify When to Discuss Development

When you face hypergrowth in a company, it can be especially difficult to balance a good culture if you are focused on keeping the wheels turning rather than polishing the car. When you have a good staff development program, it allows you to be proactive in identifying the key points of when staff might be raising these questions and preemptively set expectations, so you aren't caught on the back foot. Some key areas that you may inject staff development:

1. Your Recruitment Team – your recruitment team should be well-versed in the company values and growth paths of potential roles and team members whether through a Company DNA deck or a values deck. Ensure they know what management's approach to staff development is so that they can sell it.

2. Your Onboarding Process – from your orientation deck to your onboarding materials, you should guide your new team member's training and growth expectations.

3. Your Performance Materials – your performance materials, whether it's annual reviews or staff goal prompts, should naturally incorporate job satisfaction, job fulfillment, and long-term job objectives.

4. Your Staff HR – your core staff development materials should

reference growth paths or have it accessible to the team so staff can see their long term career path and start building loyalty to the idea of career growth early on.

In our millennial generation, building loyalty is only getting more difficult. Gone are the days where an employee stayed with a company for 20 years. Now you are lucky to retain an employee for five years. This means you are currently adapting to a much shorter-term focus paired with millennials with a much higher expectation of growth trajectory and timeline. You should not over-cater to their timelines but set expectations to manage and nurture it.

Consider that growth comes in many forms. This may be a title, increased responsibility (work scope and projects), or developing deeper technical skill sets (expertise skill track). Each of these situations requires different forms of communication, expectation setting, and performance management.

Building Skills Tiers and Growth Checklists

Having benchmarks to fall back on is the primary business foundation. To be able to scale your decisions and your management team, managers must have a core set of skills and markers to be able to reference to make decisions when it comes to raises, promotions, or increased job responsibility.

Skills Tiers: you can build skills tiers within your company by working against your Organizational Chart. You outline the various roles and job levels, and the expectations across hard skills, soft skills, and performance indicators of that role type. You can also set minimum performance indicators (for example, a promotion to senior means you must be with that company for a minimum of 6 months, encouraging retention and longevity).

Growth Checklists: to support management discussions you can build management questionnaires or checklists based on these now newly created benchmarked Skills Tiers, this puts a process in place to systemize a dialogue around what is expected of an employee at different stages of the business.

What If They've Outgrown Your Company?

In some cases, when you have a stellar employee retaining them can get tricky. They may have goals that are no longer sustained by additional work or titles. They may get wooed by different industries or broader responsibilities that the current company simply cannot accommodate. What do you do in a scenario like this? Usually, for a higher-ranking staff member that you are not willing to lose, the above materials go out the window. The principles stay the same in the discussions, analysis, and scenario planning, but it becomes very tailored to the individual.

This discussion must typically start to be held by upper management, someone with a strong understanding of the direction of the business, future roles or areas of expansion and match them to the candidate's suitability. If you are in a manager role, it would be up to you to raise this topic with the appropriate stakeholder and potentially pitch your team member on their behalf (or in the case where they are gunning for your job, let them fight their own battles).

Perception Management to the Team

Perception management is a step that most managers often miss out on. As a manager, you step into the role of representing the company, which means that the way you act and the things you say and do are now critiqued and judged by those around you. What sets great leaders apart is their ability to manage their perception when handling people and organizations. People will often react to what they see vs. what they hear; when you can manage your perception, you can manage the outside assessment of your ability as a leader, increasing your effectiveness as a leader.

When it comes to leadership, there are often three skills that are possessed: vision, interpersonal skills, and technical skills. Perception is rarely discussed but is vital in firm leadership. You may have the best intentions and concern for your team, but if it is not communicated in a manner that employees can interpret and understand as care, your choices may go nowhere, that is the influence that perception can have in leadership.

There are four things to consider when thinking about perception:

1. Objective perception is not impossible – each individual sees things from their perception. Managers must consider this when taking action.

2. Every person has a context – they will view things based on their history or factors outside of your control.

3. Individual values, beliefs, and attitudes affect perception.

4. The amount of energy a staff member spends on accomplishing tasks is directly related to their perception of its value (however, this value that they assume may not be the case).

Dissatisfaction comes when managers do not hear what employees say but what they assume they will say; for the employee it's when they hear what a manager says but they expect different. Consider the phrase "like a snake in the the grass". Did you see what was wrong with the sentence? Some read a snake in the grass, and missed the repeated 'the'. To counteract this, managers should use the sandwich technique or change the behavior by discussing praise, followed by criticism (or improvements) and followed again by positives and expected outcomes. You will discover that the employee's expectations change as they ignore the criticism they expect to come last.

Perception management is difficult because it requires a high level of self-awareness and sensitivity to the responses and reactions of others. You can protect yourself from biased perception by considering different points of view and encouraging those around you to offer their observations, ideas, and suggestions even those that may challenge the stated goal or outcome. This also allows you to step away from the action and take another view to make sure you see the whole picture and not just the part you find the most interesting. We often only see what we expect and can be blind to changes that do not match our proposed reality. Along with that, develop good listening skills and decisiveness to succeed and be able to deal effectively with all problems directed to you for resolution.

Performance Improvement – Cultivating a High Performing Team

Do you recall a time when you were part of a team that shared laughs over lunch, looked forward to happy hour drinks after 5 p.m., and would jump to help out a team member who was struggling? You were possibly part of an engaged and high performing team. A Google study called Aristotle measured over 180 teams to find what makes t a highly engaging team. They found that five factors mattered:

- psychological safety (do we feel that we can take risks in our team)

- dependability (can we count on each other to do high quality work)

- structure and clarity (are the goals, roles and execution plans on your team clear)

- meaning of work (are you working on something that you believe matters)

- impact of work (do we fundamentally believe that the work we're doing matter).

Groups where the individuals felt all five of these factors were able to harness the magic of teamwork.

A high-performing team has a high evaluation across leadership, team members, and, most importantly, able to hit performance markers (examples, sales targets or quotas for the team). While team size does not matter, these general tips can be applied to teams working interdependently under ten. Over ten, it turns into groups.

Personality Types in High Performing Teams

One of the foundations is getting the right personalities and skill sets in your teams. No matter how much of a great culture or environment you create, you cannot override, for example, a team full of Type A's. They will lack individual perceptions and values to effectively grow the group as a whole.

One technique is DISC profiling, a behavior assessment that centers around four key personality traits (Dominance, Influence, Steadiness, and Conscientiousness). You typically have a primary and secondary trait; for example, a team member might be a CS (C at 60% and S and 20% while D and I make up 10%).

Profiling is not meant to help you make hiring decisions, but rather to have a stronger understanding of your team's behavioral types to adapt how you help them communicate and what gaps might be showing in your team. If you have a sales team full of CS that are not performing, you might identify that the I trait (Influence, typically exhibited from those that enjoy interaction and draw energy from social situations) is missing. Sales typically being a transactional relationship-driven role might benefit from having an I on the team who can bring up the energy of the team.

You can integrate DISC profiling into your hiring on your team development sessions/processes. Having a strong team that understands how to communicate with each other, drives their teammates, and what is not effective encourages greater empathy, understanding, and collaboration.

How to Cultivate the Five Factors of Team Effectiveness in Your Team

Psychological Safety

As a manager, show engagement when a team member speaks. By actively listening, you create an environment where the team feels OK to speak up. Build values around reducing negativity and blame and create a culture of inclusion and feedback. Encouraging your team to be involved in decisions shows honesty, transparency, and leads to better outcomes.

Building Dependability

Dependability is your team knowing that they can trust each other. From showing up to work on time, meeting deadlines, and being detail-orientated, these factors encourage trust. At a manager's level, you can build these behavioral changes in your team by 1) communicating the importance of dependability, 2) setting expectations, 3) managing behavior that does not meet these expectations. By managing behavior, you create and cultivate reliability.

Structure & Clarity

Having organizational plans, development plans, and clear communication around the team's goals and objectives can help support structure and clarity. The part that many miss is a continual feedback loop. Listening to your staff and having monitoring in place can ensure that your communications created structure.

A term I like to use is 'check and balances', when implementing something, it's important to ensure you have checks in place to monitor effectiveness and to take action if it is not met. This can be applied in any situation, from performance improvement plans with an individual, to a newly released organizational chart. How do you apply checks and balances? You ensure the objectives of any change are clear; for example, if releasing a new organizational chart, the goal might be to ensure that team members can see a clear growth path. The next question you would then need to ask would be, how can we *measure* if there has been a change in perception of whether the organizational chart helps them see their spot in the expansive team and their potential development. This might be done through a survey or meetings with the team/individuals. If the answer is no, it means that additional materials need to be created.

Meaning of Work – Working on What Matters

This ultimately comes down to engagement. I've always believed that focusing on the key levers are much more important than worrying about the day to day. To create the meaning of work, the small things matter, like giving feedback and creating an autonomous environment. However, a great manager needs to create an environment that allows meaning even when you're not in the picture. So, how do you tie engagement to the meaning of work? Try to reframe your group to think like a team. If a member of your team feels their work doesn't matter, they are thinking about themselves as individuals and looking inwards too much. Individuals who seek praise or individual feedback need to redefine the meaning of contribution and value.

As a manager, you need to bring team objectives and company direction to the forefront and kill the employees' focus on 'me'. A sense of engagement and fulfillment will develop from here when they focus on the larger picture. You can do this through regular team communication and alignment sessions, encouraging facilitation and shared communication in smaller pods of the larger team. By creating the foundation of the focus on the team goal's you create a culture that starts to build itself.

Impact of Work

The impact of work is slightly different from creating meaning. The meaning of work is seeing that what you're doing fits into the bigger picture. Impact of work is the feeling that what you're actually working on is important. This is cultivated through reward and recognition programs tailored to the individual. Not all individuals receive reward and recognition in the same way, some may be monetary, some may seek words of praise or group recognition. Identifying and setting up a rewards and recognition program that covers different validation points help to cover a group's sense of impact.

Secondly is the existential impact of work, while you may feel that you are responsible for the employee's professional performance, their engagement is similar to improvement. Some see this falling under HR responsibilities, however people are people, and showing care for personal development has a direct link to high performing staff. You can tackle these conversations through frequent one-on-one's, quarterly reviews, check-in's and professional development discussions. If an employee is questioning their career path and fulfillment, this becomes a core issue that needs to be solved, before impact of work can be resolved.

Why Engaged Staff Show Accountability

Accountability has different tiers. There is accountability at a basic tier, which is accountability for a task or project. If you create a truly engaged team member, they will display responsibility at a much higher level, and operate in your team as if they were the company owner. You can spot these employees; if something urgent comes up on a Sunday morning, they are helping resolve the issue. If a project needs to be opened up at 11:50 pm, they are coming through with support.

Creating a Supportive Culture

To truly cultivate culture, you need to move beyond stating company values and statements. A culture is created by the people and driven by the people. You need to categorize and identify your team members and find your enablers, detractors, and promoters—typical categories under the NPS (Net Promoter Score) model. Promoters are highly engaged staff that might naturally display your company culture markers. Detractors are staff who may show negative traits not associated with your company culture. With a smaller team, you can easily identify these people and their behaviors. Be sure to reward the positive markers and discipline the negative, creating behavioral alignment in your group.

Bringing your team together to communicate the importance of your culture supports this at an operational level while your team nurtures the culture on a day-to-day basis.

Another aspect of a supportive culture is putting the people aspect of your team first. By identifying what energizes your staff (the activities they enjoy) and what drains their batteries (tasks they avoid), you can ensure your team is optimally charged, assuming energy levels are at 100%. It's your role as a manager to keep your unit at 80%.

Identifying Signs of Burnout/Disengagement

One of my senior managers was sitting in a room with me, he was frazzled, his voice high-pitched, he waved his hands as he blamed his team (while insisting he 'didn't want to blame anyone'). Gently, after a 40-minute conversation around some of the challenges he was facing and possible solutions (a few minutes in, I could tell that this wasn't an operational issue but rather a personal development issue), so I raised the topic of his mental health. How was *he* doing? He stuttered, he knew where I was going with this, but he was in avoidance, it was a big topic and one that opened a lot of holes. Three months later, he handed in his resignation.

See, he had been deliberating going back to his home country of England. He had a two-year-old son and was under the pressure of wanting to be close to his aging parents and wanting his son to go to school abroad. The strain of having to make this decision while performing his job was getting to be too much to handle. Burnout can display itself as pessimism, attitude shift, and overall negativity. You might unknowingly misdiagnose an employee that is close to crashing with one that needs performance management.

A staff member who is facing burnout needs *support*. They need coaching and help to bring their burnout to light (most staff who are overworked, put pressure on themselves or are in a field or position they don't enjoy won't admit to displaying these symptoms). Someone who is burnt out can find it hard to recover and on a professional level risks impacting the department's performance, communication between co-workers, and the morale of the team. Other team members can sense a negative or emotionally drained employee by the way they communicate and collaborate but are often unaware of how to deal with the issue.

If you spot the symptoms, you can start to work through the issues that have caused the burnout, slowly identifying factors, placing solutions, and monitoring whether these solutions are having any effect. Sometimes it may be more apparent in their performance.

Watch your high performers to ensure you are not making the mistake of overloading your best people as well as your low performers. Is there work indicating displays of low performance and potential burnout or disengagement?

When it comes to your A players, managers often make the mistake of continuously giving responsibilities to the same people. It's success bias; if the work is getting done well, we default to the same solution. However, this is a mistake, your A player may not raise this and you don't give your B players an opportunity to rise and prove themselves.

MANAGEMENT MINDSET & YOUR GROWTH

I have seen managers fail because they couldn't switch from an employee to a manager mindset. No matter what level you enter, becoming a manager means starting to treat the business as if it's your own. Politics, anger, attitude, these are no longer traits for you to embrace, but now are issues you need to manage and solve within your role. Sometimes referred to as an entrepreneur mindset, this encompasses more than being a manager. It accompanies the resilience, grit, and never give up attitude you need to undertake to succeed. This applies to all levels of your role, whether it's working with your team, other managers, or those above you.

A great manager can purely focus, drive, and spend energy on actions to move the needle. Emotions and ego must be killed. Of course, all of us are human, and these things do not happen overnight, but a trait that must be nurtured and developed. Spending time and energy on frustration, jealousy, or anger can lead to bad decisions and bad management.

The healthiest way to develop your entrepreneurial mindset to become a stronger manager is to ask yourself a few key questions and learn to manifest the **right** reactions in emotional situations:

1. What would I do if this was my business?

2. What is important in this situation?

3. What would be considered a successful outcome in this situation?

4. Am I feeling emotional, and why? What is the benefit of this emotion?

You might face an angry team member, staff arriving late, a passive-aggressive email, or an unhelpful response from another manager. All of these can easily lead to emotional reactions and decisions if you're not careful. By asking yourself the questions above, you can learn to refocus your frame of mind and move forward with a direction that takes facts into account.

How To Successfully Delegate

Delegation is key in the strategic growth of your team. It allows you to build and grow your team's skills and capabilities and free up your own time to focus on larger projects and more responsibility. Often, delegation can seem easy, but many managers do it poorly. Poor organization means not giving the right projects or tasks/duties to the right person, delegating too large projects or too small with poor communication, or not delegating at all.

I often see managers failing to hand over tasks to members of their team. As managers, we want to ensure quality control or worry that giving too much of what we do means that we won't have enough work to do or we are removing the impact we make in the company. It's one of the worst mistakes a manager can make. The value of a senior member or manager of a team is scalability, or their ability to increase the value of their output. Their value does not come from an individual task (like putting together an end of day report), but being able to successfully manage multiple parts of a business and delivering a result. A successful manager provides change. Too often, my managers fail to distinguish between the business's day-to-day operations and the innovation and performance of the business.

Delegating means identifying what needs to be assigned, and when, where should the work go, how to determine correct delegation, as well as refinement and results.

What Needs To Be Delegated

As a manager, when you consider delegation, start with your time. I break my time down into 5-minute intervals, where I spend my time and the impact on the business. Identify the areas where you are spending a high amount of time, with low impact/value. Next, consider, could this task be done by someone else? You should be refining this list every week and continuing to remove and refine your workflow and the flow within the team for the right distribution level.

Let's say in an average workday as a Customer Service Manager, you do the following three tasks:

1. Check the daily call and email response logs to ensure that all calls are responded to within three rings, all emails have been responded to within 6 hours, and the total number of calls and emails in this time is under 5%.

2. Run a daily briefing meeting for the team.

3. Put together training materials for frequently asked Customer

Service emails.

Which of these tasks could be delegated? Depending on the size and experience of your team, task one and three could be all or partly covered by someone else. For task one, the impact of this needs to ensure the benchmarks of non-answered queries is under 5%. You don't personally need to check this information to ensure the performance benchmark is met. Ask a member of your staff to send you this information by 4 pm each day. For task two, team morale, communication, and clarity are directly related to employee engagement and team effectiveness. A result of strong team effectiveness is increased performance and revenue. Hence task two should stay with the manager. Task three, do you have staff who are experienced with the training topics? If the answer is yes, you could partly assign this task by reviewing the most required training areas and having a member of your staff build their skills by creating training materials.

To delegate well, you not only need to be able to analyze the situation but identify the strengths of your team and any possible consequences. For example, let's say you decide to transfer task 2 to Mary ; however, you do not communicate to her the importance of reviewing the call rates from the day before each morning and keeping it in mind at all times. The call rates stop getting reviewed by you, and after a week, they jump from 5% to 20%. What is the cost of this mistake caused by poor delegation and communication? As managers, we will make mistakes and learn, but part of making mistakes is assessing the size of the potential consequences against the potential benefits. You may have only trained Mary to take over this job, but you are actually training her to be a Junior Manager and second in charge. The benefit of her doing the task correctly is she might take over 20% of your workload so you can focus on direct training with new customer service agents and increase their profit margins by 10%, which is a win for the business.

Delegating and Assessing Where the Work Goes

Another common mistake that gets made is incorrectly delegating the work to the wrong team member. This involves being a strong manager that understands the strengths of your team, the size of the task, and the potential negatives of a task being done incorrectly. Along with assessing your team's strengths and weaknesses, you should also have a strong understanding of their growth paths and direction.

Taking Mary as an example, she may have expressed a desire to move into a team management role. She has been with the company for 12 months and shown strong experience in taking responsibility, training new staff, and improving the overall process. You determine that she should take high impact / high consequence delegations and that it aligns with her future path, which indirectly supports her longevity and retention in the company (boosting your % of engaged staff and knowledge capital in the team). Correct commissioning is a strong skill in your toolbox to support coaching your staff, instead of training, delegation is a channel you can use to teach new skills in an environment where the employee learns through doing. You also vet staff based on real work activities and outcomes, building the team's overall strength.

How to Coach Senior Staff Members

For some managers, you might be in a space where you are new to the company. You will have staff who are older than you or are technical specialists. These co-workers can be more difficult to approach, and hold an arrogant stance ("what could you teach me?"). However, thinking back to team effectiveness and a high performing team,even if you do not have the technical skills, as a manager, you can help every team member develop more meaning in their work and impact their work. Coaching does not need to mean hard teaching skills but it can be approached by assisting that employee to be the best version of themselves and giving them the tools for success.

Just like any other staff member, you also identify their career expectations, what skills they want to grow, and how you can foster this. Another way to think about it is like an orchestra, the conductor does not need to know how to play every instrument but needs to know how to get all musicians to work together to create one fluid sound. Managers can get overwhelmed with self-doubt when it comes to knowing how to tackle a specialist or longer-tenured staff member. If you approach it from the perspective of giving them the tools required to facilitate growth and remove any barriers, you can be successful in your goal.

Everyone needs help; even the most skilled person can benefit from working through barriers with someone else. If not, teamwork wouldn't exist, and people would be running a lot more companies individually, which is not the case!

Your Role In Your Growth

One of the ways we can slip back into an employee mindset and not an entrepreneur mindset (taking a high level of responsibility and accountability for your actions and what's in your control) is mistaking that one of your duties is also to manage yourself. We go from someone else taking care of our growth, our development, and our salaries to being able to do that for others. It can be easy to expect the people above you to manage you and make sure that your growth is on track, but this is not always the case. As you move into management, there is an expectation that you should be monitoring and raising your concerns and helping steer the ship that is your progress and performance.

Take time to apply your new manager role to yourself and treat yourself just like you would a member of your team. Are you feeling the impact from your work, do you feel safe and a sense of autonomy, do you see your growth path, do you feel fulfilled? If you do not have the answer to these things or the answer is no, take control and manage the situation.

Managing Yourself

Identifying and Managing Burnout in Yourself

We were at a management retreat in Bali, we'd all flown in over the last day from around the world. Our CEO rented out three large villas with pools, and we were in for a weekend of bonding, management coaching, yoga, and drinks. Our new General Manager from Hong Kong arrived visibly worn, you could see the dark circles under his eyes. Even with a big smile on his face, you could see the last few months had taken a toll on him. Managing a team, millions of dollars, and the responsibility of keeping a business running and profitable had been eating away at him. I saw it again and again as new managers joined the group, they were bright-eyed and bushy -tailed in the beginning, but as the work kicked in, many were unable to manage the stress and drain of how much energy it took in management and how much it affected and spilled over into your personal and physical self.

From that point on, when I would coach young managers I would tell them all the same thing: management is 90% mental. It's not the responsibility or the team that weighs you down, it's the criticism, the self-doubt, the energy behind decisions, and the management of yourself that is energy-consuming. The symptoms of burnout in yourself are similar to those of your team, an increase in negativity, pessimism, and a lack of enjoyment in your tasks. But the approach needs to vary.

For a manager, they need to identify and handle potential burnout much faster than an individual employee, because the effects of your burnout can be much larger on the company. You can also be detrimental to the team who may notice your short-temper, your frustration, and your increased emotion or lack of emotion. You may not notice it, but your team will .

Some quick identifiers on a day-to-day basis is getting a quick 'emotional read' on yourself and your general attitude. Ask yourself, how do I feel about the company, and how do I feel about the work I do? If I am drained, can this be fixed? If you feel negatively about any of these areas, you <u>must</u> tackle it immediately and identify whether it is situational or permanent. Situational negativity is a normal human trait that may come and go when you notice a permanence in your feelings – maybe you are feeling underappreciated or lacking support. At that stage, you need to identify the steps required to turn the situation around.

Dealing With Burnout as a Manager

A holistic approach is needed to turn things around *quickly* if you identify you may be facing burnout as a Manager. One of the things I encourage all managers to do is set up a support system outside of the office, a person or group of people you can vent and rant to, without carrying that frustration around. If you are in the position to do so, seeing a psychologist or business coach (focused on both personal and professional performance) is a game-changer.

Like a medical condition, you need to assess the seriousness and the core reasons:

1. What are you feeling, and what is the timeline?

2. Are there potential outside stressors in your personal life?

3. Is there pressure in the workplace, or are there stressors coming from specific situations or projects?

You need to isolate if there is one core factor, multiple core factors, and how deep the impact and resolutions are. Managing burnout is a very individual solution, as I suggest a personal approach to really help turn things around. The one thing that can be applied is the speed at which you fix it. Not everyone needs to be back in the green zone immediately;instead, you can take a staggered approach to fix your burnout. You may realize you need a holiday sooner than originally planned, and you need to drop a few projects or remove some of the pressures in your personal life. The most critical action is the speed at which you identify the danger and take steps to gradually bring yourself from the red zone to orange and back to green.

Working in the Business & on the Business

Execution vs. strategy has two very different impacts on the profitability and revenue of a business. Many managers will cite time as an excuse for not getting results. Lack of results and improvement in your department is an efficiency problem, plain and simple. Not only should you be managing the efficiency of your team, but keeping a watchful eye on the efficiency of yourself.

For a year in the business, our top sales guy was running the department and hitting records. He alone was able to bring in $200,000 a month in sales. He was resistant to bringing in extra sales staff, and when we did he neglected their training and helping them. What is a better scenario, one sales guy bringing in $200,000 or two sales guys bringing in $200,000 each? I don't think I need to tell you that $400,000 is better than $200,000.

A classic example of an in-efficient manager is the inability to see that they should split their time between making money in the business and the activities that can generate more money for the business. You should **always** factor in activities to generate additional revenue or improvements that lead to increased profitability. This is the difference between working in the business and working on the business.

STAKEHOLDER MANAGEMENT

HOW TO MANAGE STAKEHOLDERS CORRECTLY

At all stages of management, you'll need to consider both 'managing-down' and 'managing-up.' Having the higher-ups on your side, being aware of how you're perceived can support you managing-down. Poor managing-up can mean you're spending more time defending your efforts or even putting yourself in a position to be terminated from your role for non-performance.

The two key tips I always give are straightforward in managing up: **understand the relationship** and **understand their priorities**. Just like in a romantic relationship, building a business relationship means understanding how the other person likes to communicate, do they prefer emails or phone calls? Do they prefer lots of detail or cutting straight to the point? Being able to tailor your communication style to their preferences will help you create a small win in more effective communication and presentation. Secondly, without combining the two areas – you still put yourself in a position to lose.

Most working professionals know how to adapt their working style but will often lose oversight that true managing-up, is creating value. How do you create value? You save that person's time. By understanding what key outputs or information matter to them, you can not just perform in your job, but both effectively deliver the information and the information that matters to them.

We had a new general manager starting in Ho Chi Minh, Vietnam, he was American-Vietnamese and pretty switched on. He'd worked previously in high-level positions and communicated well; however, he failed in our management team. His biggest mistake was not realizing the priorities of the CEO – which was sales. Our CEO didn't care about the smaller details, he didn't need a one page weekly WIP (work in progress) email outlining all the activities that were being done to get sales. He only cared about if there were sales, and if yes, how big? If no – when are they getting here?

By simplifying your communication to tailor exactly what they want or adapting your working style to understand how to serve this information better, you can create more successful managing-up relationships.

RESPONSIBILITIES OF MID-MANAGEMENT TO UPPER-MANAGEMENT

One of the neglected areas is the ties between mid-management to upper-management. Most managers understand they have a boss, but fail to realize that performing in stakeholder management is also a part of the job.

A key part of understanding why so many fail is the knowledge that one of the responsibilities of a manager is to execute on upper management's strategic vision. If I asked you to describe that vision, could you? If the answer is no, you have not put measures in place to strengthen this understanding and incorporate it into your work.

Understanding that a part of your role is making sure you have all the information needed to perform will help you move forward. Sometimes you may be working with upper-management that may have different skill-sets, strengths, and weaknesses. Learning to bring out what is needed in your work environment will help you succeed as a middle manager and also raise your career.

Middle management is difficult because you need to alternate between assertiveness and subordination – when managing your team, you are in a leadership position, and with upper management, you are a subordinate. Many think because upper-management is leadership, you do not have the authority to ask for what is required to perform your job. If communication is not clear, if the vision is and neither are the expectations, you can call on this. It's a strong trait that you can also build in your team to lift your management efficiency – developing a culture where the team understands that part of their role is ensuring they have what they need to execute their job and performance is part of their responsibility. This can also be referred to as ownership over the results.

SUCESSFULLY WORKING CROSS DEPARTMENTALLY

Working with other managers at the same or similar levels can be one of the most challenging parts of middle management. You will find you are both trying to achieve the objectives of your department (and also to prove your performance and results for upper management), but these are also teams that depend on each other. Finding a balance between all teams winning and your team performing at the top is not easy.

Creating strong cross-functional management teams can be beneficial to all parties. A strong cross-functional team relies on shared goals and success, as well as strong leadership.

Creating shared goals amongst teams is a good way to increase co-team work and facilitation. Larger companies may enlist management consultants or change professionals to help achieve cohesiveness, but you can do this through a shared goal system like OKRs (Objectives and Key Results). Instead of creating teams with differing success metrics – you tie multiple parts of the company to shared success. This encourages communication, understanding, and teamwork.

We faced this exact problem in the digital agency, where we had the client services team and the marketing team butting heads. The marketing team's focus was on getting their work done while the client services team wanted to make the client happy. These two things could work in opposition when a client wanted something last minute or a change to the work, but the marketing team had other priorities for the day. In this case, we changed the entire agency with all teams to focus on Marketing ROI (return on investment).

The client services team has OKRs linked to client ROI.

The marketing team had OKRs linked to client ROI.

They now shared a common goal.

Not only did we link their OKRs, but we also tied in performance reviews and ongoing learning and development discussion to these OKRs. It centered all staff around crucial actions in the business that would drive it forward while facilitating teamwork and team cohesion. This is a larger structural change that you can look to make to improve and align the objectives of each department. At a lower level, you can run activities like team bonding, surveys, or co-projects to increase physical working together. This tackles two aspects, conflicting objectives and teams who don't understand each other. Like any area of management, improving cross-functional team dynamics is an ongoing activity. You need to test, tweak and improve as you observe and review the actual dynamics and changes in your real teams.

MASTERING DEPARTMENT GROWTH AS A MANAGER

At the end of the day, a few things are black and white. There are the nice-to-haves such as a fulfilled team, strong culture and innovation, and the must-haves or the performance of the team. Which comes down to 2 key areas, what are the benchmarks for performance and where is the team performing currently. When it comes to teams that are focused around numbers this can be simple – say we have a sales team and they need to make $100,000 in sales monthly, if the team is hitting this number or exceeding by 20%, they are performing.

If you think back to stakeholder management and understand the priorities of upper management, this ties directly to understanding the team's priorities. Your drivers for department success must align with what upper management is paying attention to. Understanding the basic financial metrics of a company will allow you to structure your team's initiatives and focus.

Here is the minimum you should know:

1. **Balance Sheet** – Also known as a Profit & Loss statement, this is the end of month financial statement of the company.

THE FIRST TIME MANAGER

Typically a mid manager will not have access to this, but understanding that upper management and investors are driven by the balance sheet is important.

2. **ARR and MRR** – Annual recurring revenue and monthly recurring revenue; this is typically how much money the company is bringing in. This can be analyzed as an entire company or could be narrowed down to a particular area. Let's say you work for a car cleaning company, and the most popular service is the 'wax and polish' at $79 per clean. Management would want to be aware of what the MRR of total cleaning is and potentially what the MRR of the top-selling 'wax and polish' is. They would want to be aware of any drops in high-performance areas and what causes this.

3. **Profit Margins** – A great manager is aware of profit margins and the standard in their industry. They keep on top of how to optimize these profit margins while continuing to drive up MRR and ARR. Strong MRR or ARR growth does not always indicate that a company is making more money. For example, let's say that the 'wax and polish' car service costs the buyer $79, the cost to the company is $39, meaning the profit margin on the service is $49. Say that you make 700 sales of the $79 wax and polish service or $55,300. You have a great idea to run a promotion, and you get sales up to $100,000. However, after a closer look, you start to use a different wax because you thought it would be a better selling point. The cost to the business is now $69 per wax and polish service – bringing the profit to only $10 per service. So while you now have $100,000 in sales – the profit margin is only $10,000 compared to the

lower sales of $55,300 but a profit margin of $34,300.

As middle management, you will not be responsible for these numbers as part of the business, but you should be helping your team fulfill the top criteria of – increase MRR and ARR and increase profit margins.

If your guiding questions are correct, you can ensure your corrective actions are correct. To break it down even further, if you are looking at your team, you would ask yourself:

1. Increasing ARR/MRR – what could the team be doing to make more money? What are the direct and indirect activities that will drive more revenue?

2. Profit margin – what is costing money, and how do we reduce these costs / improve efficiency?

EFFECTIVE STAFF UTILIZATION & EFFICIENCY

One of the fastest ways to improve a team is to review and audit how well each member of the team is being utilized. If you have an overblown team, where the performance of the individuals and team is low, and the costs are high, this is a quick way to get the team back on track. There are a few initial questions to consider: Is each team member working the full hours that they are paid for? Is the output of each member meeting the expected minimums?

For some work areas, simple staff utilization is easy. Say you have a content writing team, you can benchmark each writer to fulfill 3000 words per day. If 3000 words per day is 100% efficiency, you can base your hiring and firing decisions on black and white fulfillment. If you have three writers in a team:

- Writer one writes 3500 words.

- Writer two writes 3000 words.

- Writer three writes 2700 words.

You can quickly identify that writer one is at 116% efficiency, while writer three is at 90% efficiency. If you expect that the team performs at an average of 100%, the team performance is strong. If you expect that the entire team is overperforming at 120%, the team is slightly underperforming, with writer three underperforming at an individual level.

Utilization can also be measured by hours. However, I believe benchmarking performance and output across roles and pay tiers is a strong and fast way of identifying quickly your problem areas. An easy way to have your team on the same page with efficiency is to *communicate* these benchmarks and expectations, which can come in the form of SLAs (service level agreements). These are minimum markers for how much output members should be achieving or how the team should be performing as a whole. For McDonald's, an SLA could be that all drive-thru orders must be fulfilled in under five minutes, that all walk-in orders should be received within at least three minutes. This says that one staff member should be able to complete an average of 20 orders in one hour.

CREATING A BUSINESS STRATEGY

You now have an overview of the different areas that you should pay attention to as a manager, but being a good manager vs. a *great* manager or a leader is a category of its own.

A great leader is able to fulfill and find a balance between company performance and the growth of the people and the company. A company could be increasing in profit by 20% every month, but it could also show a staff churn of 70% and speaking to the employees we see that they dislike working in the company and have nothing positive to say. This is a win-lose vs. a win-win situation.

What the 1% Do Differently

To be effective in your role doesn't require brains or skills. There is one thing that all strong leaders do and do well; they manage their energy effectively. It allows them to perform at 200% in the same 24 hours a day that each of us has. By performing effective **energy management**, this enables them to put the right amount of focus on high-value vs. low-value activities.

Some examples of energy-draining activities are typically ones that do not move the needle forward on either **driving revenue forward** or **increasing profit margin**. If you can learn to:

1. Identify where you need to spend your energy.

2. Identify areas that do that contribute to revenue or profit margin.

3. Optimize your energy to shift more energy, time, and effort towards high-value producing activities.

You will find that over time you get more efficient and how you spend your time, with the outcomes having an exponential effect.

How to Hack Your Own Efficiency

Energy management sounds simple but is difficult to master. Mastering your efficiency requires one thing – systems. When it comes to your efficiency, fixed and non-fixed variable inputs require time and energy. You can optimize time to swing in your favor by creating systems to minimize the time on the variables.

Fixed: You need to eat.

Non-Fixed: When, what, and how you eat are not-fixed.

You may introduce intermittent fasting into your lifestyle. You start your morning with a coffee and don't eat from 9 pm the previous night to 1 pm the next day. What does this achieve? You reduce time and energy spent on decisions like, what to eat, preparing food, planning if you are getting enough nutrition. You save yourself 30-60 minutes daily, but the five and ten minutes here and there that are spent to plan, think, and organize are minimized. Allowing you to spend that energy instead on the business and value-producing business activities.

Practicing Optimism

Often, the managers that I have seen come out on top are those who have a never-say-die attitude. Positivity is not the key to continuity, but optimism is. It's the secret to every strong leader and manager in the world. The ability to keep going when issue after issue comes up. To not focus on a single end-point but to enjoy the journey, is a skill that needs cultivating and building. Optimism is not fixed, there may be days you have it and days you don't – but learning to unlock it when needed is what will help you have longevity in a management career.

Many confuse positivity and optimism. Someone practicing positivity on a bad day might say to themselves, "It's going to be a good day!". This has no impactful benefit. Telling yourself it's going to be a good day, will not do anything. The optimist will say, "Today is not going well, but I'll work on X, Y, and Z, and that's the best I can do for now." An optimist focuses on what can be achieved vs. superlatives not focused on practical solutions and improvements. An optimist allows a situation to be subpar and focuses on what is within their control (the non-fixed variables or controllable vs. non-controllable). Building resilience to things outside of your control is the hidden asset of leadership.

CONCLUSION

Being a manager or in management will have its ups and downs. There is no one size fits all solution and you will think you have mastered one aspect only to be thrown a curve ball when another situation arises. Management much like sport and becoming an athlete is about refining, practicing and continuously improving. You may understand the players, the goal and the strategy but a different day might mean slightly different equipment, different weather and new variables that throw off your perfectly laid our strategy, requiring you to think quickly on your feet to reach the outcome.

To be successful in management it requires realising that there is never an end goal, and that there are always improvements that can be made, but this comes in time. Keeping a sense of resilience and always-on state of optimism will help you survive and thrive through the challenges that come your way.

www.ingramcontent.com/pod-product-compliance
Lightning Source LLC
Chambersburg PA
CBHW030526220526
45463CB00007B/2737